D1442586

ON A MISSION

Bomb Squad Technician

ON A MISSION

Bomb Squad Technician

Border Security

Dogs on Patrol

FBI Agent

Fighter Pilot

Firefighter

Paramedic

Search and Rescue Team

Secret Service Agent

Special Forces

SWAT Team Member

Undercover Police Officer

ON A MISSION

Bomb Squad Technician

By John Perritano

Mason Crest
450 Parkway Drive, Suite D
Broomall, PA 19008
www.masoncrest.com

Printed and bound in the United States of America.

Series ISBN: 978-1-4222-3391-7
Hardback ISBN: 978-1-4222-3392-4
EBook ISBN: 978-1-4222-8501-5

First printing
1 3 5 7 9 8 6 4 2

Produced by Shoreline Publishing Group LLC
Santa Barbara, California
Editorial Director: James Buckley Jr.
Designer: Bill Madrid
Production: Sandy Gordon
www.shorelinepublishing.com
Cover image: U.S. Army Photo/Staff Sgt. Michael Sauret

Library of Congress Cataloging-in-Publication Data

Perritano, John.
  Bomb squad technician / by John Perritano.
    pages cm. -- (On a mission!) Includes index. ISBN 978-1-4222-3392-4 (hardback : alk. paper) -- ISBN 978-1-4222-3391-7 (series : alk. paper) -- ISBN 978-1-4222-8501-5 (ebook) 1. Explosive ordnance disposal--Juvenile literature. 2. Ordnance disposal units--Juvenile literature. 3. Bombs--Safety measures--Juvenile literature. 4. Explosives--Safety measures--Juvenile literature.
I. Title.
TP270.5.P47 2016
355.8'251--dc23
                          2015004820

Contents

Key Icons to Look For

Words to Understand: These words with their easy-to-understand definitions will increase the reader's understanding of the text, while building vocabulary skills.

Sidebars: This boxed material within the main text allows readers to build knowledge, gain insights, explore possibilities, and broaden their perspectives by weaving together additional information to provide realistic and holistic perspectives.

Research Projects: Readers are pointed toward areas of further inquiry connected to each chapter. Suggestions are provided for projects that encourage deeper research and analysis.

Text-Dependent Questions: These questions send the reader back to the text for more careful attention to the evidence presented here.

Series Glossary of Key Terms: This back-of-the-book glossary contains terminology used throughout this series. Words found here increase the reader's ability to read and comprehend higher-level books and articles in this field.

Emergency!

Police swarmed to a movie theater in Colorado when a man attacked people with a gun. Police later discovered a bomb in the man's home.

Rap…rap…rap.

Tori Lynn Everhart shook the sleep from her eyes and dragged herself out of bed. It was two o'clock in the morning on July 21, 2012, a strange hour for a visitor to call.

Rap…rap…rap. Rap…rap…rap.

Everhart shuffled in her pajamas to unlock the apartment door. On the other side stood a police officer. "You need to change and get out," the officer barked. "There's a situation."

It wasn't uncommon to see police in Everhart's neighborhood. Her apartment building at 1690 Paris Street in North Aurora, Colorado, was located in a sketchy part of town. The police were a common sight on the streets.

"Well, can I get back in sometime?" Everhart asked the officer. "I'm supposed to be moving today."

"We're not sure about that," the officer responded. "That's not important. The situation is important."

Situation? What situation?

Words to Understand

evacuated   moved to a safe location, away from danger

glycerin   a substance used in soap making

infrared   part of the electromagnetic spectrum between light and radio waves

motion detectors   sensors that detect the movement of people or animals

napalm   a highly flammable, jelly-like substance mainly used in flamethrowers and bombs

precariously   unsteady; unstable

Hours before, James Holmes, who lived in Everhart's building, walked into a crowded movie theater in Aurora and opened fire during a performance of *The Dark Night Rises*. Holmes killed 12 people and injured 58 others by the time his guns fell silent.

Rigged Apartment

Police captured Holmes moments after the shooting, finding him in the back of the theater. Then they went to Paris Street and the apartment building where Holmes lived. Holmes had rigged his apartment with a sophisticated explosive system designed to blow the building to pieces. This was a job for the bomb squad.

Among the devices was a boom-box radio that Holmes had programmed to play music just after midnight. The music, Holmes hoped, would wake his neighbors and force someone to bang or rattle the door to get him to turn the volume down.

The shaking door would then pull on a fishing line attached to a thermos of **glycerin** that was precariously tilted at a 45-degree angle. When the thermos fell, it would spill the glycerin into a pan of potassium permanganate. The substance has many uses, including removing the "rotten egg" smell from well water.

By themselves, the ingredients were harmless. When mixed together, however, they were explosive. Holmes also poured oil and gas on the apartment's carpet to fuel the flames.

Moreover, Holmes had placed on the top of his refrigerator a box packed with six-inch shells attached to several black balls filled with gunpowder, gas, and oil. Holmes wired the box with a detonator made from a toy remote control. He put the remote and the toy car it controlled outside near a trash bin. Holmes wanted someone to find and play with the remote control car, which would have set off a blast inside the building.

A remote control car like this one was used by the bomber to booby-trap his explosives-packed apartment.

The presence of flammable gasoline in the apartment greatly increased the danger for bomb-squad technicians.

To make the situation even more dangerous, Holmes filled the apartment with bottles of gasoline, and jars mixed with several chemicals including homemade **napalm**, ammunition, and gunpowder.

Neighbors Stunned

Everhart didn't know her apartment building was a time bomb when the police called. She had lived in the 12-unit building for five years. Holmes' apartment was right above hers.

So with the help of police, Everhart and the other residents, along with those living in the surrounding neighborhood, **evacuated** 1690 Paris Street. Then the local bomb squad tried to figure out what to do.

Their options were limited. They thought Holmes might have rigged the apartment with **infrared** triggers, **motion detectors**, or pressure switches. Any of those could set off a blast early. Why did Holmes booby-trap the apartment in the first place? Did he want to divert police from the theater as he went on his rampage?

No one knew. As doctors and nurses tended to the victims of the shooting, dozens of police officers, firefighters, and other bomb-squad experts surrounded the Paris Street building. At first, police believed their best option was to purposely set off the bombs and let the building burn.

Lives and property, however, were at risk. Something needed to be done—and fast. One wrong move could be devastating and deadly. The bomb squad had a decision to make. Finally, the call was made: It was time to bring in the robot.

Later, in the final chapter "Mission Accomplished," read how bomb-squad experts saved the day. First, find out more about this dangerous job.

Chapter 1

During a demonstration of bomb-defusing tactics, the operator shows the protective body suit that helps keep these experts safe.

Mission Prep

As long as there have been people building and setting off bombs, there have been bomb squads. Their primary responsibility has always been the disposal of explosive devices. Many local, state, and federal agencies employ bomb-squad technicians to defuse bombs. A bomb technician is more scientist than cop.

It wasn't always so. Many historians say the first organized bomb squad was a hastily put together group of 17th-century guards who hurriedly tried to save a king's life. In 1605, King James I ruled England with an iron fist, which more often than not came down on the heads of the country's Catholics. He was their chief **antagonist**, and ordered all Catholic priests to leave the country.

Words to Understand

antagonist   a person who opposes another

arsenal   a place where ammunition and military equipment is stored

assassinate   kill somebody, especially a political figure

conspirators   people who plan to commit a crime

detonate   make something explode

Parliament   the supreme legislative body of Great Britain, consisting of the House of Lords and the House of Commons

First Professional Bomb Squad Unit

The first professional civilian bomb squad was established in England in 1874 when police led by Sir Vivian Dering Majendie investigated an explosion that destroyed a bridge and several cages at the nearby London Zoo. Majendie wrote the first laws governing the control of explosives, and developed various techniques for handling and dismantling bombs.

By the fall of that year, a group of angry Catholics decided to **assassinate** James by blowing up the king as he opened **Parliament** on November 5. To accomplish this task, the **conspirators** hid 36 barrels of gunpowder in the cellar of the House of Lords, one of Parliament's two law-making bodies. Their plan was to explode the gunpowder during the ceremony.

Fortunately for the king and Parliament, William Parker Lord Monteagle received a mysterious letter warning him not to attend the gathering on the day of the king's visit. Lord Monteagle informed the king's officials of the letter. They sent Sir Thomas Knyvett and a group of men—history's first bomb squad—to find the explosives.

Knyvett and his team searched the rooms below Parliament. There they found gunpowder and a man named Guy Fawkes carrying fuses and a timer. Ever since that episode, bomb squads have played an important role in solving crimes and saving lives.

Low Profile

The bomb squad generally keeps a low profile—until it is called into action. Bomb-squad technicians are always training and keeping up on the latest bomb-disposal methods.

There are two main types of bombs. The first is ordnance, or bombs built in factories mainly for the military. The second are Improvised Explosive Devices (IEDs), built by individuals.

Local bomb squads handle explosives found within the community. Military Unexploded Ordnance technicians search for and clear ordnance from military facilities, including gun and bomb ranges.

Police bomb squads defuse actual bombs and render suspected bombs unusable. They also conduct investigations after an explosion. Officers train for hundreds of hours to be a bomb technician. All have graduated from high school or have an equivalent degree.

Most bomb technicians train at the Federal Bureau of Investigation's (FBI) Hazardous Devices

School at the Redstone **Arsenal** in Alabama. Over the years, the FBI's school has trained and certified 20,000 state and local public safety bomb technicians. The FBI also has its own Special Agent Bomb Technicians that travel the world investigating explosive-related activities.

Students at the FBI's school study how to store and use explosives, combat terrorists, use bomb-disposal equipment, and work as an individual and on teams in tremendously dangerous and stressful conditions.

Many Duties

Once they are on the street, modern bomb techs have many duties. They might blow open a door so a SWAT team can storm into a building. They might help a HAZMAT (hazardous material) team clear a dangerous drug lab. They might respond to a bomb inside a vehicle. They might dispose of grenades that veterans have taken as souvenirs after leaving the military. They deal with pipe bombs or homemade car bombs made by would-be murderers.

David Spraggs, who spent weeks training at the FBI facility, became a bomb-squad tech because IEDs have become major problems for local law enforcement. These bombs are easy to make, and the directions can be readily found on the Internet or in books.

"I just didn't realize how easy it was to purchase the chemical(s)…necessary to manufac-

This explosive was made professionally for use in industry, but homemade devices similar to it are causing problems around the world.

ture high explosives," Spraggs wrote in *Police Patrol Magazine*. "A trip to Sally's Beauty Supply, Wal-Mart, and Home Depot, and we were good to go…one reason I wanted to join the bomb squad is that the threat is clear."

That is why most bomb technicians spend many hours studying homemade bombs and how to disarm them. Their training, more often than not, pays off. Such was the case, when New York City's bomb squad rushed to the heart of Manhattan after receiving a report someone was trying to **detonate** a car bomb near Times Square.

Several people saw smoke coming out of a Nissan sport-utility vehicle (SUV) on the corner of 45th Street and Broadway at around 6:30 P.M. They called police, and officers called the bomb squad. When bomb technicians arrived, they found the inside of the SUV packed with a homemade bomb made from three propane tanks, two five-gallon jugs of gasoline, a clock, various electrical devices, and a canister of gunpowder.

Donning protective gear, the squad broke the SUV's rear window using a robot to see what was inside. Squad members rendered the home-made device harmless and carted the SUV away.

Like all bomb squad techs, members of New York's bomb squad had been trained to stay calm. They put their experience and schooling to work in identifying the type of bomb that was in the SUV, and the best way to dispose of the device.

Text-Dependent Questions

1. What is an IED?
2. Name two situations in which the bomb squad might be called in to help.
3. How many incidents did Canadian bomb squads respond to between 2007 and 2012?

Research Project

Pick one of the cases in the text and write a report about it.

Chapter 2

The scene at the finish line of the Boston Marathon was calm a year after a deadly bombing struck the 116th running.

Training Mind and Body

Chris Connelly went to work early on April 15, 2013. After all, this was a special day in Boston, the day of the city's famed marathon. Before the race started, Connelly, a sergeant with the Boston Police bomb squad, and members of his bomb-hunting team began looking for explosives in trash cans, cars, and store windows along the route where 500,000 spectators were gathering to watch nearly 25,000 runners.

By the start of the race, Connelly declared the route clear and went to his post near the finish line at Copley Square in the city's famous Back Bay section. Other team members took up their positions elsewhere, each standing ready to respond to any situation. For hours, the technicians remained alert, looking for suspicious packages, individuals, cars, or anything else out of the ordinary.

Words to Understand

billowing   moving outward into the air

claustrophobic   fear of being in closed-in places

instinctive   based on natural impulse and done without instruction

procedure   correct method of doing something

21

Triggering Mechanisms

Bombs can be triggered in a number of ways. Bombers can use modified cell phones connected to an electrical firing circuit. They can also use radio-controlled devices, in which a signal from a transmitter causes the receiver to trigger a firing switch.

Suddenly, at 2:50 P.M., Connelly felt the ground and air shake. Then he felt it rumble again. He then saw a cloud of smoke **billowing** into the sky. Connelly ran toward the smoke, pushing his way through the crowd of people, many of them dazed, hurt, and confused.

Connelly knew what had happened: Two bombs had gone off. He looked and saw the street and sidewalk were littered with bags and packages—all potential hiding places for another device. He **instinctively** reached for his knife and began cutting the bags looking for more explosives.

Ripping through the bags with a knife was not standard **procedure**, but Connelly knew it had to be done. There was no time to call in the bomb squad's robot, x-ray machines, or remote-controlled tools to take a careful look at each package. He cut, and cut some more, later telling a reporter what he was thinking as he sliced bag after bag: "I'm gonna die. One of these is gonna be real. But that's okay. If it goes, it goes. That's just the way it's going to be today."

Looking for bombs usually is a slow and careful process. Technicians spend hours taking apart a single device. If the device is armed, it takes longer to defuse. Safety is the watchword.

Crime-scene experts swarmed to the Boston bombing site after bomb-squad experts had cleared the area.

Real or Hoax?

On the day of the 2013 Boston Marathon, those rules went out the window as Connolly's crew cut through dozens of suspicious bags. All knew one wrong slice could kill or injure them. They relied on their training and experience. Connelly would soon learn that someone had made two home-made bombs using pressure cookers. Those devices had taken the lives of three people and injured scores of others.

April 15 was a vexing day for Connelly and his men. Bomb squad technicians have to be mentally tough and physically ready to deal with any challenge. Learning about the technical aspects of locating and diffusing bombs is one thing, but preparing yourself mentally for what happens if things go wrong is quite another.

"I got my first pipe-bomb call after the first week out of school," remembered bomb technician Thelmetria Michaelides in an interview with Policeone.com. Michaelides works for a fire department in Maryland. She spent weeks training at the FBI's "Bomb School" in Alabama. Still, she says, she was nervous during her first call. "You don't know if it's real or a hoax . . . [You] have to treat every call as real."

Another challenge was donning the heavy suit and

helmet that shrouded Michaelides in a seemingly protective cocoon. The suit weighed 125 pounds. Luckily, Michaelides isn't **claustrophobic**.

"If you cannot stand to be in such a tight space, it won't work," she says. "You're going to have to wear that suit at some point." Moreover, a person has to be physically fit, which is why Michaelides works out in the gym daily. It also helps her to relieve stress.

The massive helmet worn by bomb-squad experts sits inside a high protective collar. A face shield allows for viewing while providing some protection.

Ready to Work

Bomb techs generally have to complete various tests to make sure they are mentally and physically prepared for the job. Students also have to take tests to demonstrate that they can solve problems, endure physical hardships, and have a tolerance for working in close quarters.

One of the major challenges is that technicians do not know what a call might entail. They might have to pick up ammunition left in a house, or dispose of military ordnance. They can be called upon to look for bombs on a parade route or when a dignitary visits. They search for bombs at sporting events and concerts.

Technicians might find bombs concealed in just about any container. A device might be sealed in a shoebox, a suitcase, or a backpack. It could be stuffed into a trash can, or under a sewer cover. Alone or as team, technicians have to work every case as if a package contains a bomb.

Such was the case during the Boston Marathon bombings. After the bombs exploded there, bomb technicians from a number of units, including the Massachusetts State Police, converged on the scene. The blast had torn the leaves off nearby trees. Restaurants, which had been packed with diners, were now empty as people scattered into the street.

Moreover, the bombers had yet to be caught. State police trooper Jeremy J. Cotton, a bomb technician, remembers being fearful that other bombs could explode. Perhaps, Cotton thought, the bombers would target the bomb squad techs as they worked. Cotton could hear cell phones go off in the distance. He fretted that one of those calls could set off another bomb.

"In the back of my mind, I was thinking about the yet uncaught bombers targeting us as we worked," he told *The Republican*, a newspaper in Springfield, Massachusetts. "Were they calling the phones trying to set another bomb off? I blocked it out and continued to work."

Soon after the blasts, local, federal, and state bomb technicians met at a nearby hotel to

Post-Bomb Investigation

Once a bomb goes off, experts have to figure out what happened. Things don't disappear after an explosion. They fragment into tiny pieces. Experts have to find and assemble bits of bombs, a painstaking and time-consuming task. They have to be patient. They need to know the size of the bomb, how it was made, and how much power it had. During training, bomb technicians are often required to put together and assemble a blown-up truck to get a feel of a post-bomb investigation.

coordinate plans. When it became apparent that no other bombs were about to go off, technicians fanned out to process, or look for evidence.

"It was our job to dig, sift, locate, mark, and categorize absolutely every shred of evidence we could find in the most intricate detail possible," Cotton said. "As we learned the names of the dead, the victims, the injuries suffered, it became personal, and we were hell-bent on making sure we did the best job we could."

At one point, members of Connelly's crew found a bag near the initial blast site. The bag was so suspicious-looking that technician James Parker wasn't about to cut into it. Instead, he put on a bomb suit and x-rayed the package with a portable machine. Inside were a textbook and a heavy metal tube with wiring.

With cool heads and steely nerves, the techs rigged a water bottle with an explosive charge and put it near the suspicious bag. They then detonated the bottle. The blast echoed between the buildings on Boylston Street. The package, however, did not contain a bomb, only a camera.

Better safe than sorry.

The Boston bombing was a mass-casualty incident, a "post-blast" investigation, and a live bomb case rolled into one. Sgt. William P. Qualls told a reporter, "We'd been training and preparing for something like this for a long time."

Text-Dependent Questions

1. How many spectators were along the Boston Marathon route in 2013?
2. What is a "post-bomb" investigation?
3. What agency does Sgt. Chris Connelly work for?

Research Project

Research the bombs used during the Boston Marathon bombing, and describe in an oral report how police were able to determine how the two bombs were made.

Chapter 3

A major step forward in bomb defusing was the creation of robots that can be operated from a safe distance.

Tools and Technology

At about 8:30 on the morning of September 5, 2012, Aurora Barrera walked into the bank where she worked with a strange device wrapped around her neck.

She told her astonished coworkers that three men had kidnapped her earlier from her home in Huntington Park, Calif., just outside Los Angeles. The device they placed around her neck, she claimed, was a bomb. If she didn't rob the bank, she feared, the men would blow her to bits.

With the help of a stunned and frightened bank employee, Barrera emptied the safe of $565,500. She tossed the money out a side door. Moments later, a vehicle raced to the bag of cash. The car stopped, a man grabbed the bag, and sped off.

Barrera, however, still had the bomb around her neck. The Los Angeles County Sheriff's Department bomb squad rushed to the scene.

Words to Understand

ceramic   heat-resistant material made by a mixture of clay and other materials heated at high temperatures

culverts   channels that carry water under a road

deployed   put to use, usually in a military or law-enforcement operation

fiber optic   thin cables made out of glass that can carry electronic information

nimble   agile

projectiles   objects that can be fired or launched

31

Not all bomb scares are new. Bomb squads are called when long-buried ordnance is uncovered, such as might be found at the site of a battle.

Police surveyed the situation and determined the best way to diffuse the bomb was to let the squad's robot pry the device loose.

The robot did exactly that. Not long after, police determined the bomb was a fake. They also figured out that Barrera lied when she claimed that she had been kidnapped and forced to rob the bank. Police soon arrested Barrera and her boyfriend. A judge sentenced them both to prison.

The robot that the police used that day was just one of a number of tools in their bomb-disposal arsenal. In the old days, experts relied on wrenches, screwdrivers, and other tools to disarm and dispose of bombs. Over the years, however, the technology has become more sophisticated as bombs became more elaborate. These days, bomb-squad technicians have a wide assortment of gadgets to help them do their job.

Body Armor

One of the most important pieces of equipment is the blast suit, or bomb suit. The suit is designed to absorb the bits of shrapnel an exploding bomb might produce. The suit acts like a catcher's mitt, stopping the **projectiles** in mid-flight. It also absorbs the shock wave from an explosion.

Most bomb suits are stitched together with overlapping pieces of Kevlar, foam, and plastic. Kevlar is a fabric developed in 1965 for use in tires. Scientists soon discovered that Kevlar could be woven into suits to create a type of body armor. Kevlar's fibers are not only strong enough to stop most pieces of flying shrapnel, but they are also lightweight.

In addition to Kevlar, many suits are made from a fire-resistant material known as Nomex. Blast suits also come equipped with a **ceramic** "trauma plate" that protects the area just below a technician's waist. A second plate covers the chest.

In case a bomb goes off and the blast propels the bomb tech backward, a special plastic support sewn into the back of the suit protects a person's spinal cord from injury. Bomb techs also wear special helmets that can weigh up to 15 pounds.

The only exposed parts of a bomb tech's body are his or her hands. Bomb techs do not wear gloves. Their fingers need to be **nimble** enough to disarm a bomb. The suits do not have any communication systems because the transmission of a radio signal might trigger a bomb to explode.

Portable X-Ray Machine

X-ray machines are vital tools for seeing what a bomb tech's eyes cannot. However, unlike the bulky machines a patient might find in a hospital, bomb techs use small, portable x-ray devices they can easily move and operate. They use the machines to peer into trash cans, backpacks, bags, suitcases and many other containers.

The machines have to be tough, and light enough so they can be moved not only by a bomb tech, but also by robot, or by truck. Since most bomb investigations are slow, the machines need batteries that last a long time. Moreover, the images produced by the machines have to be clear so bomb techs can tell what is inside. The best x-ray machines are those that can be set up easily.

Robots

They look like something out of a science-fiction movie: steely devices with a claw and eyes, microphones, tracks and wheels. Robots are a bomb tech's best friend and are often the first in harm's way. The machines, most no larger than a grocery store shopping cart, can do many things.

Since the machines weigh only several hundred pounds, a bomb tech can control these brainy devices remotely just as a child would a radio-controlled car. Yet, bomb robots are not toys. They are equipped with cameras,

The robot operators can use these claw-like hands to grasp parts of the bomb, cut wires, or lift the entire bomb and carry it away safely.

Tank-like treads on bomb robots help them navigate any terrain so that they can approach bombs while people remain safe at a distance.

a microphone, speakers, and a mechanical claw that techs can use to disarm bombs, clip trip wires, or safely remove a container.

One of the most popular robots is the Mini-Andros. It can climb stairs, and motor across ditches and **culverts**. It can move easily in tight places. The operator of a Mini-Andros can control the device by radio signal or through a **fiber optic** cable. The Mini-Andros is small enough to fit in the trunk of a car, and its arm can lift 15 pounds. Near the arm are two low-light video cameras. It is also equipped with an infrared camera.

Bomb techs often use the robot's communication system to speak with people. They can also mount a shotgun on the device, as well as a water cannon (used to disable bombs) and a window smasher (to gain entry into a building). The Mini-Andros is about three feet long and costs between $40,000 and $60,000.

Bomb-squad experts say smaller robots work better than larger bots. A small robot can access tight spaces, such as the aisle of a bus or an office-building hallway. They can be rapidly **deployed**. An officer can carry one in a backpack.

Bomb-Sniffing Dogs

Manuel Ynid, a police officer in the Philippines, was investigating a bombing in the city of Zamboanga. The explosion didn't kill anyone, but Ynid wanted to make sure all was safe.

As Ynid was approaching a cardboard box, his partner, Diego, a bomb-sniffing dog, alerted his two-legged partner that something wasn't right. Just as the officers moved quickly away from the box, it exploded.

Diego had picked up the scent of a chemical called ammonium nitrate coming from the shoebox. The bomber detonated the device using a mobile phone. Neither Ynid nor Diego were injured, although the dog, a 13-year veteran of the police force, was given a week off from work.

Ion Mobility Detectors

These handheld units look like a cordless drill. They literally sniff the air looking for tiny bits of explosive chemicals. If the device finds even a trace, a red light will go off.

Bomb-sniffing dogs are trained to detect explosives. The Bureau of Alcohol, Tobacco, Firearms, and Explosives (ATF) runs a 10-week training course for would-be canine bomb sniffers.

Trainers teach the dogs to sit each time they encounter a suspicious odor. Trainers then reward the dog with a treat after the animal detects an explosive. To sharpen their skills, the dogs have to learn to sniff out an explosive placed on a revolving wheel that also contains food. The dog learns to ignore the food but not the explosives.

Bomb-sniffing dogs must have a nose that knows. They learn to detect thousands of ingredients that might be used in explosives. Some bomb ingredients smell more than others.

Fire in the Hole!

What do experts do if they find a bomb or some other type of explosive? Bomb techs often put an explosive device in a containment vessel, which is

built to withstand the blast. Sometimes they have to transport the device in a special truck to where the vessel is located. It can be a very hazardous journey! After they have placed the device inside the vessel, usually a large cylinder, they then put high explosives on top. They'll ignite the explosives, destroying whatever is inside the vessel.

A containment vessel is so thick and large that explosions inside do not damage it.

Text-Dependent Questions

1. What is Kevlar?
2. How large is a Mini-Andros?
3. Why are small robots preferred over large ones for bomb work?

Research Project

Use the Internet and the library to find pictures of bomb-squad robots in action. Research each of the situations and write a caption for each picture.

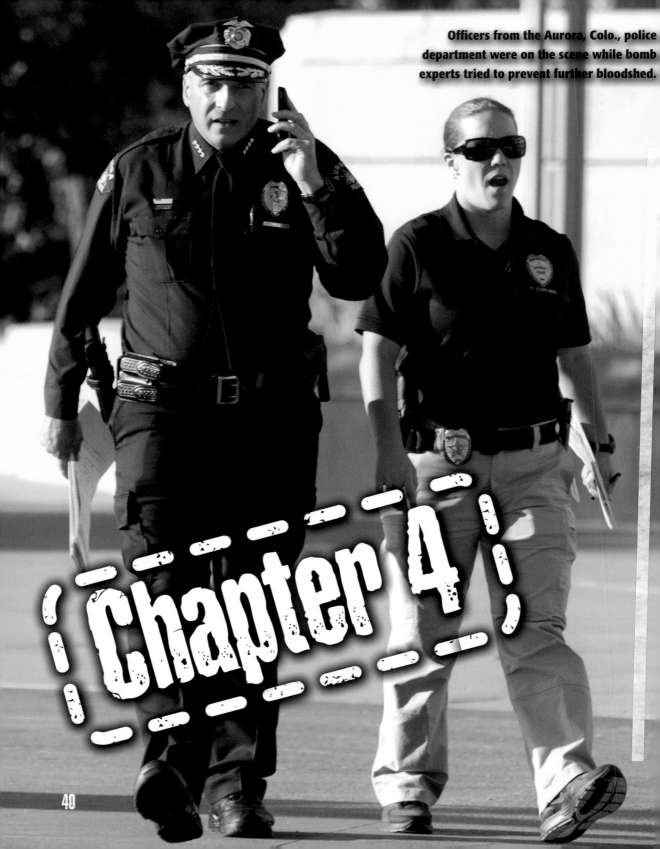

Chapter 4

Mission Accomplished!

When Lt. Thomas Wilkes of the Aurora Police Department first arrived at 1690 Paris Street, he didn't like what he saw. Wilkes, who was in charge at the scene that day, worked quickly to coordinate the actions of all first responders, including local and federal bomb-squad experts. All of them crowded near the now-vacant brick building and thought about what to do.

Holmes' apartment was on the third floor—hard to reach, but not impossible. Bomb techs cautiously climbed aboard a fire department bucket truck, smashed an apartment window with a long pole, and photographed the inside.

What they saw shocked them. Scattered throughout were IEDs, fuses, wires, and bottles of chemicals that would turn any explosion into a raging inferno.

Words to Understand

doused: drenched with a lot of water

neuroscience: study of the human nervous system

neutralizing: making something ineffective

"If these had gone off in that small an area," Denver police bomb-squad member Paul Capolungo later told reporters, "it would have been devastating."

As police studied the pictures, they became concerned that Holmes had taken biohazardous or radioactive materials from the nearby School of Medicine at the University of Colorado at Denver. Holmes attended the university hoping to achieve a PhD. in **neuroscience**. No biohazard or radioactive materials were ever found.

Police also saw a trip wire that they believed would trigger a chain reaction setting off multiple explosions.

Yes, Lt. Thomas Wilkes did not like what he saw.

The explosives were difficult to defuse. Wilkes thought the safest course of action was to set off the bombs and let the building burn. Then Wilkes thought better of it. If that were to happen, he asked himself, could firefighters protect the other buildings in the neighborhood?

Finally, using information obtained from Holmes himself, the squad made its move. About mid-morning on July 21, police blocked traffic in

every direction. They pushed everyone back to a safe location blocks away. Then the police lowered a mechanical robot from the Adams County bomb squad through the broken third-story window.

The robot, skillfully driven by one of the local bomb techs, moved through the small apartment to the front door. There, the robot found the trip wire.

The robot dropped a small device and backed away. As police officers huddled behind their vehicles, a bomb tech sounded an alarm and yelled "Fire in the hole!" The tech then detonated the bottle. The blast blew the trip wire to bits at about 10:40 A.M.

A major incident such as the one in Aurora calls for help from many agencies. The bomb expert from the Bureau of Alcohol, Tobacco, Firearms and Explosives joined others in finding the right solution to the crisis.

The broken windows and fluttering blinds in the bomber's apartment were a small price to pay for letting experts have access to the bomb inside so they could defuse it.

The robot then took a ride around the apartment, searching for computers or other things that it could remove before the bomb experts walked into the apartment.

The robot's cameras revealed a minefield of explosives. Scientists and investigators from the FBI's Critical Incident Response Group watched as the robot scanned the apartment. There were containers with chemicals, bullets left to explode, and 30 shells filled with gunpowder. Holmes had wired homemade grenades to a control box in the kitchen. The robot sprayed water on the box, **neutralizing** it. Holmes had also placed gasoline in glass containers to fuel an explosion.

The complicated setup tested the skills and experience of bomb techs. One wrong move would be disastrous. "Imagine that fireball," one official said. "You would have an explosion that would knock down walls. That flame would have consumed the entire third floor."

With the trip wire now gone, bomb techs put on their blast suits and helmets and cautiously walked inside the apartment. They methodically defused one bomb after another. They removed all of the booby traps that Holmes had left behind.

Later that afternoon, the bomb squad took all of the explosives they found and trucked them to a disposal site. They put the explosives in a trench and **doused** them with diesel fuel. They then set the fuel ablaze, igniting the explosives and rendering them harmless forever.

"This apartment was designed to kill whoever entered it," Aurora Police Chief Dan Oates said later. Thanks to the robot, bomb techs, police officers, and fire crews, a tragedy was averted.

More than 30 hours after being told they had to evacuate their apartments, the residents of 1690 Paris Street returned home.

All was safe.

Find Out More

Books

Esposito, Richard, and Ted Gerston. *Bomb Squad: A Year Inside the Nation's Most Exclusive Police Unit.* New York: Hyperion, 2007.

Fine, Jil. *Bomb Squad Specialist (High Interest Books).* New York: Rosen Books Works, Inc., 2003.

Gordon, Nick. *Bomb Squad Technician (Torque: Dangerous Jobs).* Minneapolis: Torque, 2012.

Web Sites

Federal Bureau of Investigation, Counter–IED Operations
www.fbi.gov/about-us/cirg/hazardous-devices

George Metesky: New York's Mad Bomber
www.crimelibrary.com/terrorists_spies/terrorists/metesky/1.html

PBS Bomb Squad
www.pbs.org/wgbh/nova/robots/

U.S. Navy, Explosive Ordinance Disposal Technician
www.navy.com/careers/special-operations/eod.html

Series Glossary of Key Terms

apprehending capturing and arresting someone who has committed a crime

assassinate kill somebody, especially a political figure

assessment the act of gathering information and making a decision about a particular topic

contraband material that is illegal to possess

cryptography another word for writing in code

deployed put to use, usually in a military or law-enforcement operation

dispatcher a person who announces emergencies over police radio and helps organize the efforts of first responders

elite among the very best; part of a select group of successful experts

evacuated moved to a safe location, away from danger

federal related to the government of the United States, as opposed to the government of an individual state or city

forensic having to do with crime scene evidence

instinctive based on natural impulse and done without instruction

interrogate to question a person as part of an official investigation

Kevlar an extra-tough fabric used in bulletproof vests

search-and-rescue the work of finding survivors after a disaster occurs, or the team that does this work

stabilize make steady or secure; also, in medicine, make a person safe to transport

surveillance the act of watching another person or a place, usually from a hidden location

trauma any physical injury to the body, usually involving bleeding

visa travel permit issued by a government to a citizen for a specific trip

warrant official document that allows the police to do something, such as arrest a person

Index

Photo Credits

Newscom: UPI/Gary Caskey 6, 40, 43, 44; UPI/Matthew Healey 21; Dreamstime.com: Masezdromadari 9; Brad Calkins 10; photopriti30 12; Scott Griessel 17; Mbastos 20; Billy Gadbury 25; Chamazinga 30; Frenc 35. Shutterstock: Miriam Doerr, 32; Mine Safety Health Administration: 36; Victor Griges 39.

About the Author

John Perritano is an award-winning journalist, writer, and editor from Southbury, Conn., who has written numerous articles and books on a variety of subjects, including science, sports, history, and culture for such publishers as National Geographic, Scholastic, and Time/Life. His articles have appeared on Discovery.com, Popular Mechanics.com, and other magazines and Web sites. He holds a master's degree in American History from Western Connecticut State University.